Here, Then Gone

POEMS BY

BILLIE BYRON BENTON

Here, Then Gone

© 2017 by Billie Byron Benton
"The Snapshot" © 2017 Margaret Perryman
Cover Illustration © 2017 by Billie Byron Benton
Cover Photo by Lu Ann Daniels
Back Cover Photo by Lori Benton-Janetta

Book design by SeaGrove Press

ISBN: 978-0-9993218-1-2
Library of Congress Control Number: 2017952810

Printed in the United States of America

SeaGrove Press
638 Sunset Blvd
Cape May, New Jersey 08204
seagrovepress@gmail.com

DEDICATION

For Ronald Rollet, author, teacher, publisher and friend,
whose artistry and support have enabled me to see beyond my
limited vision and without whom this book and the others I
have written would not have been born or published.

ACKNOWLEDGMENTS

I am thankful for the people who, directly and indirectly, have
supported and encouraged my writing endeavors through the
years.

In years past, the Rev. James Smith for his dramatic sermons
written to portray Biblical characters,

Dawna Markova, for her inspired use of language, both
written and spoken,

Dick Olney, for his creative and healing words, especially in
his therapeutic trances,

More recently, Thomas Moore, for his depth of spiritual
insight, his gift of expression and his words of appreciation for
my poetic writing,

Ronald Rollet, for his generous statements of the worthiness of
my writing,

Also, for poets whose works I am currently reading, Rainer
Maria Rilke, Billy Collins, John O'Donohue, Norman Rosten,
Abbott Small and Robert Bly.

And, as always, I am deeply grateful to Margaret, my beloved
wife and soul mate. Her unwavering support enables me to
continue my creative work.

TABLE OF CONTENTS

TABLE OF CONTENTS

TABLE OF CONTENTS

PRELUDE

THE SNAPSHOT

by Margaret Perryman

Billie, his mother and father
beam happily from the frozen
black and white snapshot.

There is no glimpse of the
drunken man screaming, the
cowering wife or the terrified
child peeking from the stairs.

They stand in WW II splendor,
forever fixed in a state of bliss.

No one speaks of the night the
boy is sent scurrying to the
neighbors because his father
is threatening to shoot them all.

Scrapbooks of photos hold the
history of our lives.

I don't think they tell truth.

I

ODE TO BILLIE

WOUNDING AND HEALING

To be alive and real is to be wounded,
for how else can it be?

Birth and life bring wounding.
Miraculously, there is an innate force
of healing deep within that seeks
release and empowerment.

Equally mysterious, the very wounds
themselves contain the seeds of their
own unique healing gifts.

BILLLIE SPEAKING

"You know, I tried to be someone else
for so many years, in so many ways.

It never worked well,
but I tried anyway."

THE TURTLE AND I

On this exact date eighty-two years ago, Mama's water
broke, an awkward phrase at best. I was breach birth,
born before my time, feet out first ready to run, the
rest of me more than reluctant to be pulled out of the womb.

I pleaded, "Just a few more months here in this warm
sea of safety, would be fine thanks."

But no, hands grabbed my spindly legs, tugging and
pulling. I held on and held on, except in panic I also
gasped for air, wanting to stay and needing to go.
So, like my ancient forebears, I was ejected from paradise.

As I look back over these many years, it seems that
a pattern was established, in its willy-nilly way. Slow
of pace, needing more time, feeling pushed from behind
and pulled from the front, I move with the speed of a
turtle and am apt to stop, pull in my head, legs and
feet and stay a spell.

Fortunately, family and friends give support, allowing
this turtle to eventually find his way. To add another
wrinkle, in these latter years, an old crotchety grinch
comes to visit more often than wanted. Somehow, we
are making room for him also.

So, the turtle and I give thanks with unbounded
gratitude to you, family and friends, for your love,
acceptance and support.

ODE TO BILLIE

I am floating in a therapy pool, carried
by my beloved Margaret, New Age
music dreaming its own trance, years
peeling away, becoming younger and
younger, mind following body,

donned in the clothes of birth, baby's
cry clutching throat, in wee voice,

"Did I hurt you?"
"Who, me Margaret?"
"No, you Mommy."

Soothing voice,
"No, you didn't hurt me.
It's all right, little Billie.
I love you."

WRESTLING

"Billie. It's your turn, come down
on the mats, wrestle with me."

My therapy friends shift their attention,
eyes riveted on my halting progress.

Gerry, our therapy mentor, all two hundred
fifteen pounds, was there, kneeling, waiting.
With heart pounding, stomach jumping,
feeling nauseous and sweaty, I edge
toward the mats.

Gerry announces, "I am your father."
I wrestle with him, pushing as hard as
I can, yelling my anger and hurt.
Exhausted, I stop. Gerry urges me on.
I push, I yell, I push, I yell until I
can't push or yell any more.

"Now wait, Billie, see what happens next."
Lying down on the mat, I wait. A pressure
builds. It builds and builds. It won't be
contained. It bursts it bonds.

I cry and cry. Through tears I wail,
"Dad, why don't you love me just as I am?
Why do I have to perform, be special, be
perfect? Love me! Accept me just as I am!"

Tears subside, I look up and see the faces
and caring eyes of my beloved
Margaret and our therapy friends supporting
me with their touch and presence.

There is space and peace in my belly.

DEAR DAD,

Your love is in my breath and bones.
Eighty-three years ago you and mother
conceived and nine months later the
miracle of birth was received.

Then, as happens in our human form,
caught in the hell of your alcohol addiction
and other demons that haunted you,
wounding occurred and reoccurred.
That pain, eaten, metabolized and
transformed has been one of many teachers.
Your love is in my breath and bones.

There is also much of me that is in you,
positive from your teaching, gifts
absorbed without my conscious leading.
Your love is in my breath and bones.

Without your awareness, you gave me
your blessing and sent me on my way.
I have found fathers along the path,
each showing me what I needed to know.
Your love is in my breath and bones.

Mentors continue to appear
until the path itself is clear,
becoming my inhale and exhale,
until the fathers without become
the father within.
Your love is in my breath and bones.

Thank you for your life
and for giving me mine.

Love,
Your son, Billie

OLD BEAR AND THE SACRED CAVE

Medicine Woman speaks, "Today we will ride to the sacred cave. The spirits have blessed us thus far. Your preparations are for this moment. We will chant and drum and when the spirits give their sign we'll saddle our horses. I will lead. Remember your offerings of tobacco and sage."

I fumble, having trouble cinching the saddle. Shasta, my horse waits patiently. "Old Bear, hurry up! We're waiting!" I look up Oh, he's talking to me. I'm still not used to my medicine name.

More narrow switch-back trails up the mountains another thousand feet or so. Horses stumbling on loose rocks every so often. I look to my right, straight down several hundred feet, heart in my mouth, knees shaking. It's been five days, still not used to this.

My heart beat slows, as I settle into the comfortable gait Shasta has chosen, visions of the last few days form and reform.

Our Therapy Tribe gathering from the four winds. The bus ride up the Rockies to the ranch, our first camp fire, chanting, drumming, entranced as we entered our Vision Quest, dreaming of dangers and challenges we will encounter. All of this, to discover what it is that we seek most to fill our deepest need.

I am jarred our of my reverie by Shasta's momentary stumble on a loose rock. He quickly recovers, in his sure footed way.

Scenes again appear as I reach down, pat Shasta on his neck and say thank you. I am still safe in the saddle.

Medicine Woman consulted her mentor, an old shaman, before we began our Vision Quest. He warned her to seek the spirits' blessing for safety and success on our journey.

Following his directions, we rode narrow mountain trails up to high ground at eleven thousand feet. Medicine woman found the place where the earth was shaking and eagles were flying. Dismounting, we formed a circle, chanting and dancing until the spirits' presence filled the air. Bowing to them, we offered our prayers for their blessing and our safety, leaving offerings of tobacco and sage at the points of the compass, north, south, east and west. The ceremony over, each inhale was filled with sacred presence, each exhale, a release of peace.

My aching knees and quivering legs bring me back to the present. Medicine Woman has sent word that we are approaching the cave. She and her assistants have gone ahead. They have given their offerings of tobacco and sage to the spirits of the braves who stand guard.

Upon arrival, we are to look for a sign indicating that the spirits have given their permission for us to enter. We tether our horses, approaching the mouth of the cave on foot, climbing the remaining distance. We sit alone or in twos or threes, waiting.

Word has gone out that the signs for us to enter the cave are a rainbow and an eagle overhead.

Margaret and I sit in silence. I wonder what the cave will disclose? What is it I need most to reclaim? My mind has no answer. I grow restless. The ants of unease crawl in my belly.

"Look! There it is!" a voice rings out. We look up at the patch of sky between high boulders. A rainbow. No rain has fallen, yet we see a rainbow. Another voice, "There! There's an eagle!" Our eyes follow its flight across the opening of sky.

Medicine Woman sounds her drum, telling us the guarding spirits have given their permission for us to enter. There are candles to light the way.

Awed by rainbow and eagle, I sit entranced, tension increasing. One at a time, our tribe enters the cave, each waiting until the one before has made their exit.

When the way is clear, trembling head to toes, I climb and crawl my way to the opening. Bowing to the guaradian spirits on the right and on the left, I enter the anteroom, a holy place, sacred symbols painted on the walls.

As my eyes adjust to the candle light, I see a ledge, sit down and present my offering of tobacco and sage. I pray, trembling words echoing my trembling body.

"Show me what I need to know.
Take me where I need to go".

Through a blur of tears I see the outline of the passage-way into
the cave's inner room, a birth canal. I stoop and crawl into the
womb of this sacred place. Standing, I breathe in the symbols on
these inner walls.

I am outside of time, in some eternal place, my state of being
suspended, without reference to the sensible world. There are
whirlwinds, mighty oceans and endless sky within. Nature's power
gathers its force.

I become aware of sound bursting its bounds, louder and louder,
until it fills this sacred place, bouncing and reverberating from
wall to wall, room to room, until each echo is an echo of itself
over and over again.

Susprised, astounded, I hear Old Bear growling and growling,
Each more powerful than the last. Old bear has found his power!
It has been lost a long time!

Impatiently crawling through the birth canal and bursting out of
the cave, I run, find my beloved Margaret. We hug and I cry until
there are no tears left.

THE VISIT

I was in the presence of an older man,
lines of life etched in corners and
crevaces of his face, laugh lines also
clearly visible.

His cobalt-blue eyes sparkled, inviting
me into their calm depths. He introduced
himself as Bill. Interesting, I thought,
same name as mine. Despite his age
Bill moved with ease.

His cottage, on the bluff of a hill,
overlooked the ocean. Nature's wildness
and beauty flooded in through its many
windows.

Yet, a sense of order and quiet purpose
flowed out, pouring themselves on
surrounding land and sea.

Bill spoke more by his presence than
his words. In the mornings we sat awhile
on the front porch, drinking tea.

He seemed to breathe in sky, sea and the
fruits of the soil, then exhale eveness and
peace. As I sat with him, I began to follow
his breath, in and out, inhale and exhale,
finding an unfamiliar inner calm.

My older companion moved easily through
each day, from one task to the next, doing
whatever was needed.

We weeded and watered the garden, cleared
 a path through forest brush and mended a
fence. When tired, we rested until ready for
the next activity.

Bill had a way of feeling in to find direction.
He was engaged with his present experience,
neither the weight of past mistakes and losses
nor foreboding about possible future catastrophes
occupied him. Instead, there was simply
the peace of being present.

As time to leave my older companion arrived,
I realized that in the deep places of my soul,
I wanted to become like him, to reside in the
presence of each moment.

And then, some thirty-two years ago, taking five
easy breaths, I slowly came out of trance, looked
around the room with peeled eyes. Everything
was bright, lucid with light and color. I looked
into the shining faces of my therapy brothers
and sisters.

Finally, I gazed into the twinkling eyes of our
mentor, Dick Olney, and thanked him for this
visit with my older, wiser self, knowing that
I would practice living this way.

HEALING VISION

THE BLESSING

Running full tilt, I return to the village,
greeted by my father, the chief,
with mother beside.

Both smile, giving a warm welcome.
"Son, your mother and I are here to
launch you on the next crucial step
of your life, your vision quest.

It's not without trials, danger and scare,
yet take it you must. You have been
training long and hard. The time is at hand.
Mother and I have words and gifts to
guide and protect you along the way."

Mother steps forward with a mischievous
smile, reaches behind her back and produces
a bubble pipe and a small bowl of soapy water.

She playfully blows bubbles. "Son, this is
for your enjoyment and fun. As you will
discover, it may also be of strategic use.
Here, you try."

I take the pipe and dip it into the bowl.
As I blow bubbles, I am startled to find
myself lifted three feet above the
ground. I float about ten feet and then
gently land. I blow bubbles three more
times, laughing harder each time. I
thank Mother and turn to Dad.

"Son, my gifts to you are a new bow,
quiver and arrows. The bow is made of
strong supple yew, the arrows are straight
and true, the quiver is of the finest elk hide.

Come Billie, I'll run with you until its time
for us to part."

Running together, side by side, over hills,
through meadows and forests, we chat and
laugh, at times testing each other with bursts
of speed.

In time, we come to a bluff overlooking a vast
expanse of land, to the north, south, east and
west as far as the eye can see.

Dad looks at me with solemn eyes, tears
glistening at their edges, he raises his arms,
extending them wide, indicating the land
in all directions and in chanting voice
he intones,

"Son, you will be a healer and teacher for all
people in the lands as far as your eyes can see."

We chant and dance together, then embrace.
Dad, having given me his blessing, returns to
the village.

With tears flowing down my cheeks, I pick
up my gear and run into the vision quest ahead.

HEALING VISION

THE LOOM

Father shakes my shoulder, "Wake up son.
First light is just now shining above the hills.
I have some goat's milk, cheese and berries
for us to eat. Our loom is ready, impatiently waiting."

I snuggle down further into the warmth of the
elk hide skin and blanket woven by mother for
my last birthday. Father shakes my shoulder
again, gently but more insistently, "Not today son,
We barely have enough time."

Oh, alright, I think to myself. I throw off the
covers, shivering in the early morning cold.
Pulling my clothes on as fast as I can, I splash
water on my face from the rain barrel and run to
Dad. We gobble down the berries and cheese,
taking the skin of goat milk with us.

Walking together quickly, we enter the main
room of our adobe house. Our prized loom
fills much of the space.

We talk excitedly, words race each other to find
their destination. Having decided the patterns and
themes days before, we hurriedly choose our yarn.
Dad chooses earth tones, shades of brown, dark,
medium and light, one with a red hue, a dusky
yellow and another, more golden. I choose bright
red, yellow, orange and varied shades of blue.
We marvel at our good fortune to have this valued
loom, each of us able to weave, together creating
one piece of tapestry.

We begin, fingers flying, warp and weft following
each other in quick succession, shuttle moving so
fast, it's almost invisible. With rapt attention, time

galloping on, our stomachs tell us it's time to eat. Surprised, we look up, the sun is high in the sky.

We pause to eat our noonday meal. The pattern is beginning to emerge, colors weaving together creating startling contrasts with quiet spaces in between.

Eagerly, we resume our work, pausing momentarily now and again to step back and let our eyes take in the total effect of our effort. We make changes as our eyes direct.

Time again finds its wings. Suddenly, it seems, it is hard to see. We look up, dusk is here. Just a few more rows, shuttle flying! We finish!

Dad and I stand, shaking hands and fingers, we stretch aching arms and legs. I step back and can hardly believe my eyes. Colors shout and dance together. Zig zag patterns chase each other with increasing tension. The energy of it all excites me. I begin to chant and dance. Dad joins and soon mother adds her voice and drum beat.

Exhaustion overtakes, quiet descends. Surely our entry in the village pow wow tomorrow will win a coveted place in our tribes celebration.

Dad and I embrace. Together we create! Together we are strong! Together we belong!

JAGGED ROCKS

The jagged rock and boulder laden
water of childhood has long since
tumbled and flowed its way to
the waiting sea.

Or has it?

THE PENULTIMATE

All tools are pathways,
each revealing its own
particular aspect of truth.

After they lead us there,
we set them aside
and simply experience.

MY SPIRITUALITY

I live in the temple of everyday,
for it is the common experiences
that breathe holiness,

plain, often daily acts, water
coming out of the tap each
morning when I first wash my
hands and brush my teeth,

the words of early greeting
that sound from my beloved
as she passes me on her way
to the bathroom,

the making of the bed each day
and the turning down of the
sheets each night,

and all of the space in the middle,
from dawn's light to sunset's night,
the minutia of the day's passing,
each breath, each movement, all
sacred moments, unique,
unrepeatable in their passing
seemingly insignificant splendor.

An awareness of breath passing the
nostril gates, filling the lungs,
stretching the diaphragm, with resulting
release, muscles relax, tension is expelled
and space is created.
Inhale, receive
Exhale, release

Inhale, hello
Exhale, goodbye

Without breath, there would be no life,
Without breath, there would be no death.

Each breath, a sacred moment,
a blip in the infinite that will not happen again.

Look to that which is smallest, of least importance,
most humdrum to be an incarnation.

The God that indwells most apparent is hidden
and disguised, clothed in that which is so pedestrian,
that people pass by with eyes that see, but do not
recognize and knees that bend, but do not kneel.

I pick up my toothbrush, water cascades from the open tap
and the day's holy rituals begin.

II

NATURE REVEALS

A FLASH OF BEAUTY

I stepped out on my patio this morning,
a flash of beauty flew by, a streak of
blue, zig-zagging from tree to tree,
skipping branch to branch,
visibly hidden, so quickly here, then gone.

I am grateful to have glimpsed this
flash of blue, thankful for brief moments
of beauty that dazzle my eyes and
enlighten my soul.

FALL LEAF TRIP

Seurat has been out painting
in his pointillist style,
dazzling points of light,
contrasting hues, side by
side, vibrating with harmonic
dissonance, setting eyes
aflame and stomachs quivering.

NATURE'S SOUNDS

It is 1am,
I awaken to the rhythm of rain,
nature's percussive sound.

Tonal melodies play their varied beats, arias
without words which now are soft and sweet.

Though moments ago, as I swam up from
the depths of dream's sleep, there resounded

against my window pane, a storm-fury of
drum beats with wood-winds howling and
growling their counterpoint,

welcoming us to the first symphony of the season,
evidently scheduled early this morning, the day
after autumn's equinox.

Such is nature's way to surprise and confound,
giving joy to all who open to the music of
such wondrous sound.

AN INVITATION

Today it is raining leaves,
trees unclothing themselves,
displaying yet another guise
of their beauty,

multicolored leaves strew
the ground, gems of nature
to behold. They greet the
receiving eye, opening the
gateway to the waiting soul.

Squirrels chase and play, inviting
us to join in the fun and lightness
of this autumn day.

Apples and cider, cool crisp air,
hoblins and goblins beckon and tease.

Pumpkins, jack-o-lanterns, witches
and ghosts, all waiting for us to
dance, gambol and play.

NEWS OF THE DAY

Gazing out from my breakfast nook,
I pause. What kind of topiary is
nature fashioning?

Years ago, it was but a sprig
of mountain laurel.

Today, my eyes are drawn to
a creature of considerable size,
nearly six feet, with flowers ablaze,

massive head held high, with
legs and muscular thighs,
its tail waving in the breeze.

I wonder where next it will travel,
what adventures it will have and
whether it will return before,
once again, I sit with cereal bowl
and spoon awaiting the news of the day.

THE CARDINAL AND I

I sit again in our breakfast nook,
a flash of red streaks by and
for a brief moment lights on
a nearby branch.

In the blink of an eye
Mrs. Cardinal, muted in her
rusty red coat, is adorning
a neighbor's bush.

Before I have time to exhale,
she is off to the next brief stop
in her flighted journey.

My wandering mind glimpses
how alike the cardinal and I.

NO MATTER WHAT

White oak before my eyes,
I remember, when after
hurricane storm, your
branches on the ground lie,

though scarred and stunted
with top of trunk sheared off,
you remain determined to
reach up high.

Now, looking up, I see a
branch some twenty feet in
the air, waving welcome
amidst its own patch of sky,

with thanks for your persistence,
no matter what.

RUMPLED LEAVES

Rumpled leaves dancing in autumn wind,
myriad colors flashing in their own
syncopated time,

earth-tone russet reds, muted ochers,
bright yellow cadmium and lemon light,

all now making their winded flight,
landing in yards, front, sides and back
until all are carpeted with their sensuous
gifts and smokey scent in brisk, crisp air,

inviting all to come and play
on this magnificent autumn day.

GIDDY BIRDS

Poems, like a flock of giddy blackbirds,
fill the air with incessant flight,

chitter-chatering, sky replete with black
bodies and wings, lighting on trees,

pausing for half-a-breath or so, then
off to other branches, some in flight,

others momentarily still, tree tops
adorned with their restless ornaments.

Suddenly, trees empty, sky darkens
with specs of black and quiet calm descends.

The poet, catching his breath, puts down
his pen and smiles contentedly.

COYOTE

The shadow of coyote on my friend's
front porch. Shy! Leaving his skat!
Waiting for just the right moment to
make his presence known.

Wildness in the midst of a country
suburb. Polite, to a point. Not
wanting to disturb the peace of
the land.

Yet needing to bestir the surface
calm. For underneath, life's
disquieting disclosures await.

BOOTHBAY HARBOR, MAINE

I am sparkling blue water,
reaching from one continent to another,

hilly wooded shores, mountains, valleys,
meadows and grass, with birds swooping
and soaring in clear salted air.

I am boats, sailing to the freshening wind,
zig-zagging among fir-treed islands
dotting my bay.

I am fog creeping in, here before you know,
roiling, billowing, so thick your don't see
but a finger ahead, inviting the surprise of discovery.

I am teeming with lobsters feeding hungry
stomachs with meat sweet and tender,
the smell and taste of the salt sea and air.

I am waters where whales breach and play,
then raise their tails to sound the depths,
while on the next rocky isle, seals sun themselves,
singing their barking melodies, diving and
cavorting in the surrounding sea.

I am lighthouses perched on the tips of
islands near and far, continuing to save
lives, guiding boats to safety, keeping
them from rocks and shoals.

I am here, inviting you to come, open to
wind, waves and sea, blueberries, lobsters
and fish.

You will be refreshed and your soul will be fed.

PATTERNS IN THE AIR

Butterflies on wings creating
their own patterned flight,

crocheting delicate doilies,
lovely lace filigree to behold,

one minute there,
the next, gone with the air.

III

FOR FUN

MIDNIGHT'S MORSEL

In the middle of sleep, I become aware
that I'd just eaten a poem.

For the most part, it was a tasty morsel,
except for the last sentence of the first
stanza. It was actually a bit tart.

Then there was the first line in the forth
or was it the fifth verse? It was a bit salty.

I was just polishing off the seventh line,
when I heard the sugar cookies begin to sing.

In the end, they turned out to be the most
delicious of all.

Perhaps, I will awaken to discover that
the poem I ate was a dream. Except I am
filled with a most wonderful round,
contented feeling in my belly.

I drift off, wondering if yet another
tasty morsel will appear?

OH, LITTLE BIRD

As I drive into my carport a little bird
lands on top of the lawnmower handle.

I immediately begin negotiating, "Oh,
little bird, what would it take for you
to agree to mow my lawn?

You are perfectly perched to do the task.
Perhaps you'll agree if I take a turn guarding your
nest. I'd prefer the swing-shift, if you don't mind."

"You say you're much too small for such a huge
responsibility. Not strong enough by far.

Well, you could gather your friends and then
supervise. Ten or twelve will fit on top of
the handle."

To which the bird turns, looks at me with
one eye, winks and flies away.

Maybe we could have struck a deal if I had
offered to stand guard for two shifts.

THE DAY THAT ARRIVED LATE

First, there was the sun,
though scheduled for 5:42am,
it arrived when I first opened my
eyes. I believe that was 10:30am.

Then, breakfast was set for 9:22.
It didn't take place until much later.

And most intriguing, our date
to see a movie with friends was
postponed and rescheduled for
the following week.

Finally, struggling out of bed at 1:36pm
we arrived at the diner for our breakfast
at 2:04.

I have already put my order in for
more days that arrive later than scheduled.

SNOW DAY

"I think I'll spend the day counting snow flakes."

STORIES

They sit barely six inches apart,
he, with aging gray-yellow hair
and a body paunch, dressed in a
dark blue business suit, wedding
ring flashing on left ring finger,

she, younger by far, small,
petite with streaked blond hair
after the fashion today,

both nursing drinks, hers, red wine,
his, golden brown, perhaps a single
malt, engaged in intimate conversation.

Could this be a tryst in some hidden spot,
far from the usual haunt, or perhaps a
May–December find,
or a father–daughter visit?

On second glance, more truthfully a stare,
surely love is in the air, sexual energy so
intense it isn't to be ignored,
only appreciated and adored.

ADVENTURES AWAIT

As the eyelids of day close,
the familiar world of objects,
shapes and colors are painted
with shades of night,

Day recedes into the mysterious
haunting of the dark.

A dreamworld, like falling snow,
gently blankets the well-known, so
that the most usual scenes become
exotic, luring us forward.

Adventures of night await.

IV

THERAPIST'S NOTEBOOK

THE JAGGED HOLE

As husband and wife take their chairs
in my office, a jagged hole sits between them.

The accumulated acid of years continues
to eat away, the veneer long since split apart.

Layers and layers of interlocking patterns
begin to emerge and untangle as we dive
into the well of discovery.

Will this deep water drown or cleanse?
We pray for the baptism of compassion
and forgiveness, the rediscovery of the
love that drew them together in the long-
lost years of yesterday.

We trod the prickly path of healing,
picking bouquets of roses, dark and
red, along the way, drops of blood
gather and pool as roses' thorns appear.

At each step we pause to allow the effects
of the journey to deepen and to notice that
seedlings of new flowers are beginning to appear.

HEALING WATER

I am transported as the afternoon
sunlight dances across our
backyard swimming pool.

Shimmering patterns form and
reform. Their hypnotic power
draws me into some mysterious
other world.

The weight of clients' urgent
agonies slide off my back,
slipping into this world of
light and water.

Muscles relax, an ease of relief
flows its way into the nooks
and crannies of my body.

"It's alright," the water murmurs, "It's alright.
Sunlight and healing water are there for them too."

Whether they claim it or not
is for them to do.

END OF THE DAY

I have held fragile hands with
five people today. Now, at day's
end, exhausted and more than
ready for the surcease of sleep,
my tears find me.

Vulnerable as my clients,
the shadows of their sorrows
and suffering invite mine to
surface, seeking their own
compassionate companion.

Is there that loving soul within
who will abide with me until
time has run its course?

I say yes and yes again and
find that relief and easing
from soul's deep well.

It is there within for each and
for all who will open and receive.

HEALING BALM

They sit in my office,
pain spilling out on the
floor, until the walls begin
to heave and sigh, while
both clients and I find our cry.

Together we begin the journey
through brambles and stinging
nettles, carefully placing each
step across the land mines of life.

We embrace and hold misery in
sacred space as it becomes more
visible and raw.

That from which we run,
we now hold up to the sun,
whose light cleanses with its bright.

Though, at first and from time to time,
there may be ripping pain, with chest
bent to knees in sobbing sorrow, the
miracle of acceptance and healing
doth appear.

Through storm and quiet, inner peace
is found and, most surprising of all,
this much sought after gift wells up
from depths within, unearthed through
compassion and presence.

And there are those who are so wounded
that they are not able to open to the
healing balm within. My tears and prayers
go with them.

V

DISTURBED

AMERICA THE BEAUTIFUL

There are ravenous beasts roaming this land,
 gorging on the carrion strewn about.

Wolves stalk the forest deep,
the towns and cities of our keep.

Fear mongers hawk their wares, while eyes
peer out through drawn shades and
behind locked doors people quake.

Barricades are thrown up, walls laid
brick by brick by brick, until the
protected become the imprisoned.

Others rant and rave, foaming at
the mouth with their tirades. The
gnawing heart shrivels and shrinks,
becoming a soulless stone.

What will it take to break open fear's
hard shell, to find the heart beat
of compassion still?

Must we make those who are different
the enemy, to be kept out, shunned
and sent away?

Must we repeat the ancient need for
human sacrifice, for scapegoats whom
we blame for our sins and shortcomings,

Our dire needs and tragedies, who become
the objects of our anger and hate, needing
to be banished or even tortured or killed?

This is not a plea to be blind, naive or
suicidal. To protect our nation, home and

hearth is a must, but not in some rabid,
frenzied way.

Rather, with wisdom and discernment,
to seek to protect and keep safe, while
with open arms, to welcome those who come in
need, bearing the gifts of their traditions,
humanity and skills.

We are a melting pot, including
those who are native to this land and for the
rest of us, scratch below the surface, to the
blood that flows. It comes from the world
over, from the rivers, mountains, and countries
that cover this earthen globe.

THE HEIR APPARENT

The heir apparent to the throne,
has been elected by less than
a majority of citizens voting.

In this new world, up is down and east
is west, no matter where the compass
needle may point.

Even though the unelected King
will not be crowned for several more
weeks, the cacophony of his words
resound, crashing through barriers
of soundness and sanity.

The twaddle of his twitter states
what he puts forth as fact, which
he then denies and reverses with
the next tweet, also proclaimed as fact.

The mad King elect creates his own
Alice in Wonderland. We wonder,
will we too tumble down the rabbit hole?

VI

SPIRITS SPEAK

A QUESTION

Without dark there would be no light.
I wonder if the same is true of sorrow
and joy?

SOUL WATER

Did you come to the well too soon, needing
to taste more fully of life's fair and foul?

For how could you not seek to inhale life's
pleasures and promises, imagining that
Eden is but one step away,

only to find ashes filling your mouth and sought
after heights collapsing into depths of despair.

Ah! Now you are ripe for soul water that slakes
your thirst and finds you worthy of the depths of truth.

PANGS OF HUNGER

Baby cries out, pangs of hunger
felt deep in the pit of her stomach,

Mother responds, her breasts engorge
with nipples dripping the milk of love.

With embracing arms, mother cuddles
her beloved and baby suckles

with intense need, lips pursed tightly
drawing life-giving milk from
mother's liquid body, both swimming
in love's deep sea.

After the feeding a radiant glow
beams from mother and child,
filling all space around.

It's warmth touches those who
enter the room, penetrating body,
heart and soul.

It is for all to know, that each is
mother to the child who dwells
within and who, from time to
time, cries out from fear, want
and need, waiting to be embraced,
protected and fed.

FIREFLIES AND FIRELIGHT

Fireflies and firelight twinkle
this night against black sky,

Mirroring the stars sparkling overhead,
inviting an answering response,

that we may show our flickering light,
joining together to share compassion,
truth and sight.

LOVE'S LIMITS

No one can guarantee the safe passage of another,
no matter how desperately wanted, to spare the
spikes and thorns that stab and impale, is more
than one human can do for another.

Yet, how hard we try, husbands, wives, aunts, uncles,
brothers, sisters, and especially mothers and fathers.

For those we love most, we can protect and defend,
even offer our lives as ransom.

Yet, in the end, while accepting the love and protection
of those who compassionately care, each is responsible
for their own survival and well-being.

THE BEAUTIFUL MIRROR

There is a mirror that I pray you
and all will be able to see,

the mirror of what you have been
and can be, the smudges and smears,
the blemishes we bear,

for we are all clay, soil of the earth,
and thus, we are meant to be.

Nevertheless, we are also heaven's
highest dream.

Within each, there is a heart able to
contain the suffering and joy of every
creature and fellow being,

For our hearts and souls are bound together
with all who have been and ever will be.

This is our life and destiny, to be
joined in compassion and grace,

seeing the mirror reflection of brother-
sisterhood embedded in the core soul
of each.

FICTITOUS TRUTH

As I read this novel, the rhapsody of
soundless words whirl around near space.

Unable to assign them logical sense, I give
myself over to their melodic meaning.

Transported to some nearby galaxy, light
years away, I am surrounded by mysterious
beauty which transforms and enlightens.

Truth is told, but not understood, yet there
is a cleansing and healing release, the
price of a gift waiting.

TIGHTWIRE

To be out there on the tightwire of unknowing
is both exhilarating and daunting.

EASTER

There is a smile in the sky
and laughter dancing in the wind.
Tears have been shed in months past
and surely will again.

And today there is a smile in the sky
and laughter dancing in the wind.

Yet, how often we see through blind eyes,
with extended cane in hand, tapping
here and there.

And many times our ears, deafened by
cacophony loud and insistent, hear
only the sound of their own silence,

while all around music resounds to
bear us heavenward and beauty
abounds to delight and astound.

When will the feather-light brush
of red cardinal's wings become
visible to shuttered eyes?

When will our deafened ears hear
the symphonies and sonatas in the air?

When will our receptors open
to what is already here?

When will our blind eyes see
and our deaf ears hear?

Today, there is a smile in the sky
and laughter dancing in the wind.
Tears have been shed in months
past and surely will again.

And today, there is a smile in the
sky and laughter in the wind.

BOUND, YET FREE TO BE

There is a freedom and a binding in
conception, transported in semen and ovum,

given shape in the cataclysm of love's
mating, carried in mother's womb,

safe, warm, protected and held captive,
yet free to grow and to be.

RE-CREATION

Upon leaving our daily responsibilities there
is a subtle relaxing, a refreshing letting go,

muscles release, emotions gentle and the sea of
the soul calms to the sound of a soothing sigh.

VII

MUSIC OF LIFE

TRANCE

We sit in the Main Street American Cafe,
entranced by the Dan Burke Acoustic Band.

Two middle-age Babes are bumping hips,
swaying and singing.

The sea of sound surrounds. We float
high and dive deep.

Lyrics and music transport us, creating
timeless travel to distant shores,

until as one, we stand, clapping and shouting,
not wanting the trance to end.

At the urging of Carmen, soulful supporter
and promoter, the band plays an encore.

Again, we breathe deeply, inhaling the
delicious sound, continuing the journey
until the song ends.

Then resurfacing, we awake, refreshed and fulfilled.

THE BLUES

Danny wails! Words tumble out!,
soulful, sad and sweet.

His guitar wails back, the conversation
joined, ripping and tearing, 'til hearts
bleed life's blue song.

Drummer, rhythmically sounding,
pounding and beating, relentlessly
pulsating until the tender sore place opens.

Mouth-harp sighing, moaning, soaring
until, out of the depths, bitter-sweet
words form, "Oh God! Can I bear it?"

The body responds, exploding with energy,
coming from some primitive place, moving
beat by beat, until the trance of life overtakes.

There is just.... There is just......
That's it! There is just.......

THE RELEASE!

Over and over..... AS THE BLUES WAIL ON!

MUSIC OF LIFE

With every word that I write, I hear music.
The notes flow and float their melodic
path, lyrical in the way they discover one another.

The themes and counter-themes appear, each
stating their truth, answering one another, the
warp and woof of the opus being woven,

light and dark, each taking their place in the
emerging composition. Sometimes brass lead,
other times, wood-winds, with the bass providing
foundation and percussion establishing the rhythm,

interweaving, yet going their own way,
pushing and pulling against each other,
only to come together as one piece of
cloth, whole and intact.

I wonder, as both words and music
unfold, if you too hear? Not the same
words or melody that find their way
to my ears, but rather, those that sing
the songs of your soul.

If you haven't yet heard, I beg you,
open to the melodious sounds that
live within, the symphony of your
soul, uniquely yours and yours alone.

VIII

TO HONOR

LEADING THE WAY

For Becky

You were the first, leading the way.
Your Mother and I fumbled and
stumbled, not having received a
guide book that day.

From the beginning, you were
determined, and determined you
have stayed, to fight and find your
own path, no matter what barriers
before you lay.

Many rocks and boulders have
appeared to challenge and dismay,
yet some-how you persist, taking

a step, then the next and the next,
bearing scratches and scars as
they come, you nevertheless
emerge with life vision intact,

with a smile that is radiant, even
when shining through tears.

You will continue to find your
way, giving and receiving,
guided by your love, faith and
compassion.

YOUR WEDDING

For Becky and Lee

Becky and Lee, you come to each other
in the fullness of maturity, your eyes
and hearts open.

With compassion and caring, navigating
the seas before you, serving others in
need at your door, you give according
to your call.

Inevitably, there are sunny days and
storms that befall. Together you will
weather them all.

With God's love and yours, you will
find joy well deserved, strength in
full supply, lasting and everlasting
until day's final passing.

CELEBRATION

For Lori

Healing and healer,
in a natural and flowing way,

wherever you are, in whatever
context life puts you, you
connect with others in a

caring and compassionate manner,
interweaving your life with theirs.

Over your fifty-five years,
the warp and woof of this
tapestry has blossomed so that
it covers the great halls of your life.

Blessed in the love you and Jody share,
together you grow a garden of
compassionate care, tending every

flower, valuing each for its unique
beauty and aroma, whether tulip,
carnation or rose.

We celebrate your birth and life
and the gifts you bestow.

SHARDS

For Becky and Lori

In the years of our first family constellation,
before Margaret's time, sharp edged shards
smashed our family's path for many years,
littering the way.

Drops of blood formed their own patterns
from shard to shard, sometimes coalescing
into pools, staggering their presence between.

Through the years healing artists, found
deep within, have appeared. Each of us
willing to heed, has found our unique
canvas and medium.

Slowly, painfully, the shards discovered
their way into a mosaic. With startling
intensity, clashing hues portray vitality
and life. Others floated their way into
sparkling sky and sea, each with
calming balm.

I give thanks for you Becky and Lori,
artists and healers, that you continue
to bless this earth with your lives,
hearts and souls.

TRANSLUCENT BEAUTY

For Barbara

The translucent skin of her face
shone gracefully, holding the
treasure of the dark wine of her life.

Whatever the aching tears bespoke,
agony and regret, mistakes made,

there was a deep well
of peace, stretching the skeletal skin,
opening to the grace of forgiving love

and the claiming of her own gifts
of healing and new life, she richly
bestows upon the hurt and maimed
who come to her open door.

X

MORE LOVE SONGS TO MARGARET

SOUL SPACE

Dear Margaret,

Having finished a late lunch,
we sit together in the diner
reading our books, at times
in silence, comfortable in
wordless space.

In the background music plays,
a time warp, love songs of forty
years ago, our first meeting and
love, when the heat of magnetism
and passion found a way, even
when there was none.

Now, many years later, the lines
of age etched in your face and
mine, we sit in deep pools of
soul space which nourish and fulfill.

Love,
Bill

COMPANION OF MY BEING

Dearest Margaret,

Oh companion of my being,
lay with me in eros and
urgency this living day.

May the sun's searing flame
consume our presence,

so that as twilight dims
the day and welcomes the

dark of night, our two souls
become the ashes that remain

and then reawaken as dawn's
tender light beckons us once again.

Love,
Bill

STATELY GRACE

Dearest Margaret,

Your presence radiates a stately grace.
Solid rock anchors you, flowing

waters surround, dancing with
lightness and laughter, fed by
springs of compassionate tears.

Touching others and being touched,
gifts of love and delight.

Thank you,

Love,
Bill

HEALING PRESENCE

Margaret and I stand in some unfamiliar
place, arrived there in some unrecognized way.

Golden, calming light pours down, music
surrounds and sings its depths in our souls.

We breathe deeply, inside and outside
intermingle, until there is only the harmony of what is.

A familiar voice greets us,
"Welcome little sister,
welcome little brother."

Tears well up in our eyes, and pour out,
refreshing the earth and blossoms at our feet.

Our beloved Mentor's voice in our ears,
his presence before us, we bow in
gratitude for the reuniting.

Somehow, words are not needed.
We are, once again, encircled,
sitting in the sacred space, with
our brothers and sisters.

Dick's drumbeat and bass voice
chanting their entrancement.
We join, one following another
until our souls are united in
their holy seeking and celebration.

Slowly, quiet descends. Sacred space
has opened.

One by one, we sit with Dick,
opening to receive the balm that
heals the wounds of our hearts and souls.

As the magic of healing happens, each
is joined with the rest, until there is
the tapestry of interwoven souls,
its own masterpiece.

We are again welcomed,
"Come little sisters,
come little brothers,
Let us sit together and see
what miracles will happen."

X

TWILIGHT

CHANGES

When did I begin to have such trouble walking?
When did I stop being able to run?

Yesterday it was spring,
today snow covers the ground.

HERE, THEN GONE

Those slippery-slidy moments
of life fly by on eagles wings.

We grasp and grab, desperately trying
to stop the swiftly flowing stream,

Yet they're here, then gone
before our next breath.

ELDERS PRAY

Tears form, falling slowly,
rivulets gather on porcelain skin,

shimmering with their precious
liquid, laden with the salt of

sweat, sadness and joy mined
over many years.

The drum beat of heart's pulsating
countless times, continues sounding

life's rhythm, as we live in the
Cathedral of each day, for the time

allotted, singing praise and shouting
anger and woe, as challenges come and go.

Bear us onward to the end of our days,
increasing in depth and wisdom,
ever inward, in all of our ways.

BREAKFAST

"What do you have for breakfast?"
"Sometimes bacon and eggs,
sometimes, tears and toast."

THE GIFT

As I look out my front window, I
see the oak trees that are standing
and miss those that are gone.

Years ago, El Derrecho stormed through
and ten oak trees crashed to the ground.

I glance over at our beloved oak
rocking chair, created and hand
built by a gifted craftsman.

And I consider, that for the chair
to be made, the oak had to die.

BREATHING

Life begins with the first breath,
the first inhale, the first exhale
and then the second and the third.

Each breath that we take is a
hello and a goodbye.

Breathe in, "hello."
Breathe out,"goodbye,"

a receiving and a release,
each a rehearsal, a practice,

day after day, weeks, months,
years, following one after the

other, until they pile up, a
lifetime, then a last exhale,
a final release, and …

AFTERMATH

My pace is slower these days,
the distance traveled much less,

the degree of difficulty increasing
with each achy step.

Waddling like an elder duck,
I all the more treasure each
footfall I take.

A LONG TIME LEAVING

I feel myself leaving,
a few cells at at time,
going I know not where.

A little less energy to
propel me into the waiting day.

Fear hides around the corner to
greet me unexpectedly in its
grotesque way.

Many thoughts blow through
on hurricane winds. Feelings
cascade over cliffs of waterfalls,

tumbling and landing far below,
foaming and churning until

finding their quieting, then
more easily flow on their way.

So for now, this is the news,
only partially reported, for
the sun also shines to warm
and brighten the days.

A QUESTION

"My death hasn't happened yet,
or has it?

Perhaps birth and death arrive together
regardless of the number of years lived."

MORNING RITUAL

I slowly count the pills,
swallowing them one by one,

in the same order that I collected
them from their bathroom shelf.

I am strangely comforted and
reassured by this simple ritual.

All's right with the world.
The sun is shining and I
will live another day.

However, at times, the pills
playfully create their own order,

after arguing over which one
will go last into the mysterious
unknown of the new day.

STARRY NIGHT

When I was fifty I dreamt of sailing
the endless seas with my beloved,

hardly able to wait to gaze upon the
starry skies from the middle of the ocean.

Now that I am eighty-two, I peer out
my back window, awed by the beauty

of the infinite points of twinkling lights
that greet my wondering eyes.

AT THE OPERA

At intermission I was offered a
walker to help me up the stairs and
down the hall to the men's room.

Irritated, I smile graciously and
said, "Thank you. I'll be fine once
I get my legs moving again."

ELASTIC TIME

"Some year, some month, some day,
some night, some hour, some second
death and I will meet.

It sits on the horizon waiting
and I inevitably move toward
it in elastic time.

AMEN! HO! SO BE IT!

DREAMS OF THE ELDERS

Midnight moon casts tree shadows on the
ground. Stars and planets twinkle ancient light,

shimmering for thousands, sometimes millions of years,
visible this night for our eyes to see, beckoning us, the
elders, we who are the ancient ones.

"Come, old ones, welcome your dreams, open
to your visions, unlimited by youth's naivete,

free from the prison of the middle years' need
to succeed, to make sense of it all, as if life
were a gigantic puzzle to be solved.

Let the wisdom of the years unfold through
the wrinkles of your parched skin.

Speak to us of living in the depths of sacred mystery,
the amalgam of life's inevitable pain and tragedy,
transformed by purifying fire.

You are the gold that remains, free from the need
to pretend, opening to the miracle of that
which is actually present.

Each moment becomes dreams realized, as each
dream becomes the moment that is lived.

AN ELDER REMINISCES

An eighty-four year old friend stopped by our
table as we sat in the air-conditioned restaurant,
protected from the summer furnace outside.

Our friend recalled the days of his youth, when
his parents built the Buck Tavern, popular through
the years serving local game, deer and quail.

He bent over his cane, stooped by the years,
his face beaming a wide smile, he continued
in his jocular style,

remarking on times gone by, when he bought
his father out, married his sweet-heart and
lived in the apartment above the tavern,

overcome frequently by the heat and humidity
of Southern New Jersey's oven-baked summers,
no air-conditioned comfort back then.

With slow exaggerated movements, lifting arms and
elbows at a tilt, he grimaced with pain, then quickly

returned to his warm, inviting smile. In turn, our
arthritic bodies shifted to find more comfort.

Bent over his cane, with smile intact, our friend
hobbled toward the door. In parting, he looked
back and commented,

"They call these the Golden Years.
Truth is, they are really the Rusty Years."

LEATHER SKIN

One morning peering into the mirror,
we find leather skin, parched and wrinkled.

Suddenly, we become aware of death,
nipping at our heels, our own mortality

undeniably present, seeking an audience.
We turn away to avoid the encounter,

only to find death's twin beckoning us
onward. For if it were not for birth we

would not be facing death. Birth and death,
death and birth, two sides of the same coin.

Do we choose one without the other? An
impossible dream, even a foolish one.

For when death takes us, what will
we then be born into?

SEEKING

Though I am eighty-two, passion
burns brightly in my breast.

The fires of desire fan hot, needing
to go even more deeply,

seeking physical and spiritual
union in soul's infinite place,

to touch the eternal, yet be grounded
in the muddy clay of earth,

the finite and everlasting bound
together in mystery and grace

and I their inheritor, seeking
both solidity and space.

PRECIOUS MOMENTS

Sitting this mid-late evening in the cozy
comfort of our living room, lulled as I
rock in the gliding chair, legs and feet on

the moving foot rest, back and forth,
back and forth, creating a soothing lullaby.

And, in the haze of the distant past, cradled
in mother's arms I am being rocked, surrounded
by her singing.

"Oh baby mine, safe in my arms.
I sing you gently to sleep".

In dreamlike manner, images of decades later
appear, Margaret and I at anchor in our chartered
sailboat, swaying in the tropical trade winds,

aqua waters caressing a nearby beach with
the rhythm of the sea returning to land.

Precious moments, remembered and treasured.

EMBERS

In years past, the fire blazed so hot, it seemed
rooms ignited when the woodstove door opened.

In these latter years, as the fire slowly ebbs away,
lingering embers remain, providing a comforting
warmth for our waning years.

DANCING IN THE WIND

I sit in the early evening, as
twilight sun dances on tall oak
trees swaying in the invisible wind.

I rock back and forth in our glider chair,
looking out the picture window, my rhythm
echoing that of leaves, branches and trees.

I am awed that all nature is wed together
in reverence and belonging. And that

in due time, I will be rejoining the
invisible wind, dancing in the twilight sun.

AT RIVER'S EDGE

I sit in fireplace light gazing at the
scene before me. "Oh painting from

my hands, what mysteries are hidden
in your brush strokes and varied hues."

I recognize the limpid flowing water
on which I have traveled these eighty-two years,

and remember when I arrived at the pier
on river's edge, some forty years ago.

Sturdy oak planks provided safe entry,
a welcoming sight and an invitation
to stop and stay awhile.

Tying up my boat, I climbed onto the dock and
discovered a path through waist-high river grass.

A cottage appeared, half-hidden across the yard.
Behind the cottage, protective trees stand guard,
domed by a luminous sky.

Years have passed, a deep calm surrounds this
tableau shared with my beloved mate.

Many people have stopped to share their journey,
seeking peace of mind and soul. Upon their
leaving we are all enriched and made more whole.

When it is time, I will trod back to the pier at
water's edge and board the boat moored there,

as I once again, join the river which will carry
me to the waiting sea.

AFTERWARD

Eighty-two years in the blink of an eye.
Dawn to twilight in two seconds, it seems.

What do we make of it all?
What is the journey of life about, anyway?

Each answers in her own way.
Inevitably, we make life's journey.
We are then, the journey we live,
our own unique expression of life's meaning.

Some years ago I wrote a motto that has
been above my desk since.

> "Truth for me is to experience life
> and to express and share what I
> have experienced."

Here, Then Gone is a present expression
of my life journey.

When I was younger, I envisioned my latter
years as being the most creative and expressive ones.

I am deeply grateful that this belief has become
a reality. Five books in five years, one coauthored
by my beloved wife, Margaret and our daughter
Lori, another, a selection of eighty-seven of
my oil paintings, painted over the years.

I give thanks that the poems and paintings
that have been gestating for many years
are now pouring out.

There is a creative force within. When
heard and honored, it flows through and
we become its channel. Ego self stands
by with an incredulous look on his face,
knowing that the words and brush strokes
are beyond his imagining.

It is my prayer that my words have touched
you in a soulful way, enriching your life
journey, as you in turn, enrich others.

AUTHOR'S BIOGRAPHY

Bill, christened Billie Byron Benton, received his BA in philosophy from the University of California at Berkeley, his MDIV from Union Theological Seminary in New York City, and his MSW from Rutgers University of New Jersey. Bill has worked as a Presbyterian minister, a social worker, and a psychotherapist.

Life has provided Bill with soul deepening experiences of loss and heights of mystical discovery. It is the magic and sacredness of each person and each day's experience that inspire his work.

Bill and Margaret, his wife, partner, and soul mate, reside in Southern New Jersey where Bill has been writing poetry and winning awards for his oil paintings for many years.

www.ingramcontent.com/pod-product-compliance
Lightning Source LLC
Chambersburg PA
CBHW051815040426
42446CB00007B/679